A Seed Not Watered
The Throw Away Kid

Richard Holle

Author of
The Wisdom Tree; A Black, Brown and White Story

PublishAmerica
Baltimore

PublishAmerica has allowed this work to remain exactly as the author intended, verbatim, without editorial input.

Softcover 978-1-4560-1941-9
PUBLISHED BY PUBLISHAMERICA, LLLP
www.publishamerica.com
Baltimore

Printed in the United States of America

I dedicate this book to …..my wife, the light of my life for 56 years.

Acknowledgements

I would like to thank the following people …

Dale Arsnow
Roger Chiglo
Paul Erickson
Beverly Helleland
Herb Highum
Ruby Highum
Courtland Humble
Lynn Humble
George Ingram
Holle Jean Kelley
Ronnie Kjos
Andrea Konetchy
Gladys Manion
Betty McMahon
Marcella Rislove
David Winblad

With special thanks to…..
Joann Truss

And the following places…
Rushford Area Historic Depot, Rushford, MN
Tri-County Record, Rushford, MN……
Whalan Museum, Whalan, MN

for their contributions.

Prologue

This is not a pretty story! It speaks of a kid that just hung in there, <u>a tale of survival</u>.

A tragic turn of events led to my learning how to count while playing poker at the Whalan Tavern at three years old and by selling whiskey out the back door at eight years old. This is not your normal life. This is not your normal story.

A little guidance might have been the spark and a path to steer a young life in a direction not of selfish wants, but of meaningful achievement. Alas, after all these days this lad, now old, and yet unfulfilled is still on the quest for self-attainment.

Let us get this straight now, right now! I did not ask to be born into this world. It was not by my choice and it was not my fault. Under the circumstances and knowing what I know now, I might have voted nay.

There have been moments of great joy and achievement. It would have been a sorrow to not have experienced those times. Likewise, many bad times should not have happened and certainly would not have been missed in my human experience.

So soon in life the questions, is this all there is? Is this worth the pain? Why just go on day after day without a reason, sans a point for life? Since early in life I have questioned the value of life on a daily basis. I have asked myself, *"What is this all about? Is it worth more or less when added up at the end of each day? Cash it in or go on?"* So far I am still here, but I still weigh in each time the moon appears.

Before I am done, and before it is over I apologize. I regret putting my wife, the light my life, through the nonsense, through some unhappiness for fifty six years. She has been the single beacon of hope in my life and the only glue that held me together. I often feel it is time to cross over and I have no fear.

"You are a survivor." she often states firmly. And so it is. The sparkling eyes speak of love and truth and are the spark for me between here and the other side. She is my life and I will survive at her will.

Chapter 1

Still a Mystery

This was a personal tragedy that is not totally clear in my memory bank. It was never discussed by anyone and that is strange in itself. There are many blanks. Some have been filled in and others…..?

Many years later, I learned from my Aunt Madeline and perhaps other persons on my paternal side, about the angst or conflict between my mother, Alice, and my father's parents, Albert and Marie Holle. The problem seems to have focused on my mother.

Why were my parents married two years before revealing that status to anyone? No reason was ever suggested. It was never a topic. It was never discussed by anyone, within my earshot and neither did my father, Leonard's name ever come up in conversation all my life. That in itself now seems strange.

Leonard and Alice Holle (from the family collection)

My parents, Leonard Holle and Alice Johnson Holle, were married in August of 1927. I was an only child, born almost 7 years after they were married. Why such a long time after? The town thrived on gossip and still does, no matter how poisonous, harmful or hurtful, but all through my childhood I never seemed to hear what I know now must have been well discussed. My self-esteem was always low. Throughout my childhood I felt ….less than dirt. What instilled this feeling in me?

Chapter 2

It's A Boy!

"It's a boy!" The doctor declared in his clear bass voice. He cradled the tiny baby in his two huge hands and presented the newborn to its mother. "He is a healthy fine baby, but there is also bad news. This is your first and your last child. Your uterus will not support another pregnancy. Mother, here's your baby boy!"

Leonard, the baby's father, was the last to carry on the Holle name since he was the only son born to Albert and Marie Holle. Leonard worked at the local grocery with his father Albert, the baby's grandfather. Leonard delivered groceries in those days in an old Model T. The running board became the seat for his dog Yoyo. Yoyo went with him wherever he went. Leonard did his job with pride as he waited and hoped for a son who would be destined to be the third in line of the family grocery. His hopes were high.

Albert and Leonard Holle In the Grocery Store (from the
Holle Family collection)

The nurse maid standing by through the birth process, called
on a young friend of hers to run to the grocery store, just five
or six blocks away. "Run with the news!" she commanded.

The young boy ran as fast as he could, over the Brooklyn
Bridge to the market, burst in the front door, and shouted to
the father and son team staffing the store. "It's a boy!"

Grandfather and son hugged each other knowing the family
line would continue. The family business would always be a
part of the heritage. It would always be there.....but would it.

The grandfather a slender man with graying hair always
parted in the middle and clothes always neat with the white
shirt pressed and often sporting a bow tie, gave a positive

gentle nod to his son. "Go!" He commanded to the 30 year old son nicknamed 'Haystack'.

The young father exited at the run to 411 Grove Street.

Chapter 3

A Tragic Turn of events

Alas, the family never really got started. The family plan was to turn tragic. When I was one year old, my young father had developed a serious intestinal problem, a form of colitis. After three months in the hospital he was sent home ...to wait and gain strength for an operation. There seemed to be nothing they could do due to his weakness. There was much anguish in the family.

My father's two sisters, Madeline Chopp and Lillian Arsnow, returned to the family home on the corner across the street from the high school that they had all attended. In the big yellow house the young father lay on the daybed in the sitting room, and the life went out of his body. I was in a basket or crib just feet away from the body of my father. The ticking clock with chime announced the time and though this child had no understanding, it was chiming a milestone in my young life.

Stuckalitten. Stuckalitten. Words that are maybe without modern meaning either in English or Norwegian, were the sounds of my earliest memory. I was lying in a sort of crib with white basketlike sides restricting any movement. Occasional faces were looking down and repeating the same phrase. Family members filed past and stated their grief, "Poor little thing, poor little thing," was repeated.

I was too young to understand the gravity of the situation but I saw the faces and the ceiling as I lay in the crib. Other sights impressed upon me were the stuffed eagle on the shelf and the wooden clock with the arm swinging and ticking. Ticking still bothers me today, after many decades. Though there are many gaps of memory in my life, that event still sticks. For one so young, it was a life altering experience.

There were tears on the face of my Aunts Madeline and Lillian, as they wept. Even at this early age I had memories about the faces but none of them were of my mother. It recently hit me like a bomb; none of the faces were of my mother, why not? The sisters were distraught; they had lost their brother whose body lay on the couch in the sitting room. Where was my mother's face?

It would be the largest attended funeral in the history of the little town, out of respect for the status of the paternal grandparents no doubt.

RICHARD HOLLE

Grandmother Holle (from the Holle Family collection)

After the funeral my paternal grandmother took charge of me and that is where a problem started between my mother and grandmother.

Where was my missing mother? She was making the rounds in the bars at night. My paternal grandmother, Marie and my mother obviously were two strong willed women as opposite as day and night and were caught in a struggle over me. As a child I did not have a clue or choice. My mother clearly stated hands off; don't interfere or she would take their grandson where they would never see him again.

My mother returned to her tavern circuit right after my father's death. Just bits and pieces of her behavior and life

16

have filtered down over the years and frankly it sickens me and I can no longer tolerate listening to more information.

Chapter 4

Grandfather's Plan

It should have worked out well. A.J. must have had a game plan. A plan for 200 years and not worry about tomorrow was his philosophy.

A.J. Holle a Norwegian immigrated to the northern part of the Midwest of America and ended up on a farm in Minnesota as did most immigrants to this area. Albert became a successful farmer in the Bratsberg area of Fillmore County. Albert was never meant to be a sodbuster. Albert had imagination and a desire to achieve and learn.

Albert and Marie married in May of 1899. Their first child, Leonard was born on the farm. (Courtesy of Tri-County Record Newspaper December, 1910)

Albert was a visionary and he opened a livery stable that was a three story building. It measured 32X70 feet inside. It housed carriages, buggies and horses, a robe room, a harness room and even a bedroom for the night man.

My paternal grandfather was hard working, strait laced and a good businessman. His wife, my grandmother, was stern, strict and aloof, with hard and severe features. From my earliest memory I seldom saw a smile on my grandmother's face. Her face always seemed to sag. I have always felt it is tragic to pass through life personally empty and unhappy. Life for such people was just a passing from birth to death and occasionally an obligatory smile, one without the emotion of happiness.

Holle House(from the Holle Family collection)

Albert and Marie lived in a big house on the corner across from the school. Their house was impressive for the day with flowers, gardens and statuary. The houses in those days had a separate large summer kitchen where cooking was done in hot weather, from which came smells of Norwegian food that still linger in my memory.

Most people lived a quiet life in a small town with little recreation except what was accepted for their station but not my grandfather. Albert was an inventor, creator and visionary. For a time he was Sargent-at-Arms in the Minnesota legislator. He invested in oil in Texas and invented a grass catcher for a lawnmower.

Saturday night was their big night in town. My grandfather would back the shiny black Studebaker with the glass flower vases on the inside wall, out of the barn, grandmother would get in and he would drive three blocks, park on the main corner in front of the telephone office, and walk across the street to his grocery store on the opposite corner. The front door of the store was open with lights on. Grandma would sit in the car for two hours before the market closed, watching people pass by and nodding to those she knew. It was an approved activity for women in this male dominated society. Such was Saturday night for them in this small Midwest town.

My grandparents were obviously quite religious and on Sunday they occupied the same pew in the Rushford Lutheran Church. It was kind of an unwritten possession and nobody else ever sat in that location. There were scarce times that my grandmother must have prevailed over my mother and I sat between my grandparents in their pew; too small to see over the back of the pew in front, but hearing the words of the Reverend. It felt safe.

I ask myself now, *"Safe between my grandparents or safe in church?"* I am not sure to this day but I know I really never felt safe very often. I had been baptized in the font that still stands where it was so long ago. That wooden font, worn and discolored still is steadfastly serving many generations of the congregation.

My father was evidently much like my grandfather. I don't know if they were close but my grandfather lost heart when his only son died and so he sold the store. If my father would have lived, I would most likely have been a grocer today, the third generation, but it was not to be.

Chapter 5

A Hard working Drunk

My mother's father, however, was a different story. He was a hardworking drunk who mistreated his family. His wife, my maternal grandmother died 3 years after I was born and I don't recall ever seeing her. They had emigrated from Norway with their first of 12 children, Mary, was born on the boat on the voyage to the new land.

He was a character; my maternal grandfather. His name was O.C. Johnson but he was called "Cockeyed Ole." His right eye focused straight ahead while his left eye constantly circled about. He was a hard drinker who worked as a mason throughout all his days. O.C. Johnson is stamped in many of the old concrete sidewalks in Rushford as an epitaph to his life.

Grandma, my mother's mother was described as mean, ill-tempered and other unpleasant descriptions, and it has been said to be my good fortune to miss that part of my heritage. We lived in the same small town but I never saw her. She must have spent the majority of her life being pregnant. Alice, my mother, was the youngest of their 12 children but by the time the 12th child came I don't think Grandma Johnson cared about children any more.

I really do not know enough about her to write a description. I have no pictures of her in my mind. That in its self is a little sad.

O.C Johnson Family (only known photo of the Johnson Family)

Chapter 6

A Child Not Wanted

A few of the many local women who were described to me as my babysitters at various times and places are still living and I recently became reacquainted with them. One of them was Gladys Manion. Glady, as she was called, remembered that I liked goulash, I still do. She was my babysitter many times when my mother and Hugo went to work at the tavern. She fed me goulash that was prepared by my mother and she put me to bed. I remember her kind smiling face.

Even though there are blank spaces in my memory, there are bits and pieces, here and there that form the thread of my early life. Even as a toddler I was alone too much of the time. Almost always I was alone. I did not know where I was, who I was or anything except being alone day or night; just alone. Whether it was Christmas or birthdays I was alone. Feelings of security were never part of my life and I have never slept soundly.

Whenever Alice and Hugo were at home it was Old Gold time. The acrid smell was always present. It was the cigarette of choice of my mother and Hugo and wherever they were smoke dominated the air.

I do not know when the change occurred. It might have been gradual or it might have been sudden, but for a life time, it has been a day-by-day decision. It was, and is, a serious fight, a fight to continue or give up the ghost. Whenever this change happened, I found that I had adopted a conscious survival mode.

For the early years, it was an unconscious basic animal sense of survival. It was a struggle much of the time, but as a young child I did not have enough information to decide on the value of life. Ironically, that lack of data is the reason of continued existence today.

Early on there was little contact with what normal American family life should be. Nothing in my childhood would set an example. My mother only came to school once and that was when I was in the fourth grade. No one came to my high school graduation. I knew something about my life, perhaps everything, was different. Whether or not it was better or worse, it was my accepted and standard way of life. Surviving this long in a society with a start that was so different from the norm has not been easy and most of the time in question. I know not if the normal life style is right or wrong and I choose not to impose my judgment from the outside, where my life has always been. Foolishly I attempt to seek acceptance in a society and to do the right thing in my eyes that doesn't always seem to be acceptable to the general populace. It seems to be a dog-eat-dog society. I just do not fit. Still trying, still stupid, I keep on fighting windmills.

I came back. Yes, I came back to my hometown, but I am not here! In a strange way, after all my journeys and the myriad of experiences in my adult life, down deep there was the belief that my home town would always be there for me. I know now that it never was. It is a different place. I do not fit here. The town has not changed. I have changed. The two are not compatible. I must go! I am related to many people here, but I have no family. Looking back, it was always this way. I was alone. I lived a solitary existence in a small Midwestern town surrounded by relatives with whom I had very little contact.

Chapter 7

The Throw Away Kid

Cousin Betty really brought it to focus one day. She had come to our home in southwest Portland to visit and renew a long lost acquaintance. We spoke of old stuff, personal things of childhood. We were picking ripe blackberries; one for the basket, then one for the mouth. We had had very little contact over the years, but our mutual interest in China now brought us closer. Betty spent years teaching English in Cheng Du, China. I studied Chinese Mandarin while in the service of my country and since have continued to study and travel in China.

At one point Betty turned, looked at me eye-to-eye with a handful of blackberries in front of her, and asked "Why did everyone in our family call you, the throw away kid?"

It caught me off guard, but I replied, "It is pretty simple and yet really complicated." We were silent. We said nothing more about it.

I had lived all those years knowing in my gut that something was wrong, had always been wrong. The formative years, those first six years of my life had not been within the scope of normal. At times I did not realize my life was very different from children of my age group. I thought for one thing that everyone paid room and board at home. What a shock when years later I found out many truths.

Now I can understand Betty's question.

Chapter 8

Comfort Zone

Grandma Holle and I were in the bay window in the corner of the large dining room. I was playing on the floor and grandma was gently rocking in her chair and the clicking of her knitting needles were a reassuring sound. I was in a seldom encountered comfort zone with the sun casting a warm glow on the floor. Grandma had been glancing at the ticking clock on the shelf. She carefully laid her knitting materials on a side table, opened a small drawer and removed a hypodermic needle. She was diabetic and it was time for her insulin shot. She raised her skirt and plunged the needle into her leg. She showed no reaction and I assumed it was painless, and thus throughout my life I never had fear of vaccination.

Grandma looked at me and said, "I pray the Lord my soul to keep," repeat my words Grandmother ordered. "If I should die before I wake I pray the Lord my soul to take".

My grandmother looked into the adjoining sitting room where my father had crossed over to the other side. The daybed where he laid was still in the same location. Colitis or maybe Colorectal Cancer was the cause of death according to the certificate, though some say he drank too much and that spelled his demise. Years later I wonder if I inherited the gene from him, my mother or from my maternal grandfather who was a renowned drunk. I have a taste for wine and at times have imbibed to excess.

Mom kept her habit of making the rounds of the bars each night. She was well on her way to becoming an alcoholic. She would appear at the door from her rounds and would quickly hurry up the stairs to the room where we were staying since my father's death. There was no love lost between Mom and my grandmother. When Mom found her new soul mate in one of the taverns grandma asked if I could stay with her and my grandfather. Mom flew into a rage and screamed she would take me away and they would never see me again. It was so hard for both grandparents and especially for grandpa. It was a tragedy that he lost his only son and now the threat of losing his only grandson. His plans for the future vanished.

A good man and friend of grandpa knowing of grandpa's plight purchased the store, sadly ending the dream and plan of the family grocery

Chapter 9

Whalan

I do not know how or where my mother's new soul mate, Hugo Lawrenz, came into our lives. Mom must have found him on the tavern circuit; it sure had nothing related to church or school activities. Soon, mom married Hugo. I think they were married, although I have never been able to find proof of that marriage. Hugo never adopted me, but the three of us lived together. I don't recall that he ever really had a job except for tending bar. I think they got money from the government and sometimes they had jobs tending bar in various taverns.

At three plus, I had spent what seemed like countless hours in the back seat of the old Ford, and on this one day I had my first taste of a lifetime of travel. It was like leaving home, for the first time. I was like a ship without a sail, not knowing where I was or where I was going. I did not recognize anyone except my mother and my time with her had been seldom. Where were we going?

The same trip today along the Root River is a pleasant half hour ride from Rushford to Whalen, Minnesota. Highway 16 designated a National Scenic Byway, follows along the Root River on a narrow path between the river and the bluff. The many shades of green are dazzling. It is a mixture of mostly hardwoods with areas of conifers. Wild flowers abound. Through the trees the clear ripples of the Root River winding its way east to the Mississippi, are visible. All this, of course, totally escaped this child's notice years ago.

I was riding in the rear seat stuffed in with the few accumulated earthly belongings of the man and woman whose heads I could see above the seats in the front of the car. I could only focus on this awful feeling and I didn't know why I felt so bad. This was my very first trip anywhere and I was carsick! Adding to the misery was the pair in front who were filling the car with smoke. Old Gold I was to learn was the atmospheric source of days, weeks, months and the early years of my life. It was providing the haze of everyday sickening air. Old Gold, not Camels, was almost similar to a religion depending on the smokers. It was as if they were speaking of a deity.

Whatever the brand, on that car ride I only knew of my physical status, and I regurgitated every last ounce of the contents of my tiny torso. The woman opened the window, flicked here cigarette out and instructed the man to pull over. I immediately felt guilty. I had held back the eruption until its control mercifully exploded. As well as feeling physically ill, I immediately felt guilty. There emerged that usual feeling of being in the way like I shouldn't be there, and then to make a terrible mess! With all windows open the two adults grimaced, giggled and threw the affected clothes off to the side of the road.

We passed the Peterson Bridge three miles from home still heading west. I did not know where I was going. The large man was driving and my mother sat in the passenger seat. I was somewhere between three and four years old and was somewhat aware that the woman was my mother, although a real bond had never been established. The large man driving the old car was unknown, a total stranger. The winding road between Rushford and Whalen again brought me to absolute nausea. The driver again pulled the auto to the side of the road. He recognized the symptoms and knew it was coming. Opening the door I leaned over the side of the car and regurgitated over and over. Giggling from the two in the front seat was no help. The man advised deep breathing and relaxing. The remainder of the journey was just a blur.

We arrived in a small hamlet with a few people walking here and there. The area looked shabby, but there were signs of life. My mother's new husband turned the car right and parked near the side entrance in the rear area of the tavern that was to become home. It was a relief to get out of the car that had been so full of smoke for the entire trip.

Much has changed since that ride decades ago. Today the tiny hamlets that dot the map along the river are struggling to stay alive. Disappearance of some family farms and the advent of easy travel to larger cities with the large stores and lower prices, small businesses in the small towns are a dying venture.

My wife and I traveled without meeting or passing another car and then there was the sign, Whalen, population 64. It was still there. My right turn across the Root River bridge brought back clear memory of the first arrival to Main Street, Whalen. The few old buildings are in better condition now and the streets are clean and well kept. The tiny post office is still in operation, but with very limited hours.

Whalan State Bank (courtesy of the Whalan Museum)

Two blocks and there it was, on the southeast corner of 2nd Avenue and Main Street. The old two story building was standing starkly alone. It was once the Whalan State Bank. It also is in much better condition now and the large front windows are filled with plants and flowers. It is far different from the old days when neon beer signs and cigarette posters told of the tavern's trade. In those days there were often people on the street. Now, though much neater in appearance, it looks like nobody lives in Whalan. Once, the tavern had been a bank. Now there is no bank, there is not even a tavern.

Looking up high on the hill stands the Lutheran Church and the well-attended cemetery which has far more residents than those still breathing in the streets below. The absence of even a stray dog on the street is very telling. Quiet living is the mode for those few residents, whoever or wherever they might be or if they be. Not a sight of people or movement as in the past.

Chapter 10

Home Sweet Home

It did not take long to remove all of our earthly belongings from the back seat and trunk into the room in the back of the tavern. I stood off to the side so young and oblivious to everything happening around me. There had been changes, rapid changes in my short life and I had little concept of anything. It was a day-to-day matter of survival and responding to commands of my mother figure and the large man called Hugo. I was too young to understand life but I knew my life depended on those people. They were poor people living in a hand to mouth existence with little or no thought of tomorrow. The sum total of their belongings was contained in those few cardboard boxes which they quickly unloaded.

In spite of their plight the pair were laughing and giggling while moving into their new quarters. For them it was a new beginning. They were both occupied with cigarette in hand and smoke rising from nose and mouth. Soon, the meager materials were inside the small dark room.

Hugo asked my mother, "What about the little man?"

Though I did not really understand the words, a feeling was conveyed when my mother exclaimed "Oh, there you are! I had forgotten all about you. Come on in."

I dutifully obeyed. The room reeked of disgusting smells. This same odor would linger through the taverns and back rooms throughout many of my adolescent years.

There was an open door, covered by a curtain that led to the tavern and we went through it into a long dark room.

Mother pointed to another rickety door just inside the bar. "That's the toilet," she said, "if you need to go, go."

The tavern toilet and sink was in a small enclosure; an area that looked and smelled as though soap and water had never been used in any effort to cleanse.

Holding bladder and bowels so long I scarcely had time to open the door. The filthy commode was yellow and brown..... urine and fecal material covering the toilet and floor. There was no choice other than to relieve myself in the nearest possible place and this was it. Afterwards I returned to the back room.

Whoever had been the previous resident had vacated recently. The drawers in the two old dressers were left gaping open, empty of contents and ready for new occupants.

The tavern had been closed for a time. It had been the only watering hole in the tiny village on the bank of the Root River and now it would be back in business.

This corner bar location at the junction of the only two streets in Whalan was the only real center of local activity. The building had been a bank when the town had hope, but that hope had faded and the actual time of its demise is unknown. The handful of commercial structures lay empty. Dusty storefronts gave the appearance of skulls absent of life. The owner of the old bank building wanted to establish a business in the structure and the idea of a tavern seemed to have a better chance at survival. An old bar, wooden vintage booths, some well-worn tables and chairs and a rusty beer cooler probably all purchased from a similar failed venture were in place within a day. The lights went on, both of them! They were bare bulbs hanging at the ends of the black fabric wires turned on by pulling a string. The area was not well lit.

The two newlyweds had their first job together. It was an occupation that fit the pair to a tee and would fill most of the following years. This was a bad situation for a young boy, but it was, so to speak a roof over one's head.

It was only a couple of hours until opening. The weather was hot and sticky, and the beer was cold in the cooler. The new job for the newlyweds was nigh and they were all settled into their new home. It was time for a cold beer and a smoke, an Old Gold, of course.

The word spread and when the lighted fluorescent beer sign went on at dusk they appeared, the regulars were back! Where they came from has always been a mystery, since there had not been much sign of life before the sun set. The old jukebox broadcast "Roll out the Barrel" over and over. None of the patrons seemed to notice the repetition they just kept singing along. Outside the fireflies lit up the darkness and the "heat bugs" produced their own music. The whine of mosquitoes filled the air both inside and out. People strolling by were peeking in the front windows. Children played on the walkway under the light of the beer sign. It was as though the little town had been reborn. These were the night people.

Whalen, at one time, had been a thriving small Midwest community, but nothing is ever static. The one constant is change, or the one consistency is inconsistency. Nothing can ever always stay the same. No matter how anyone wants everything to stay forever what it always was, there will always be change. At any place in time, it will be good or bad, positive or negative and economically either up or down. Of course those measurements are only in the eye of people. And so it had been with this small town located on the bank of the Root River with Highway 16 running parallel. The bridge was like a doorway into the lives of these small town residents.

For all time, there was been little change in the number of citizenry.

Chapter 11

The Tavern

They had carried a few boxes of belongings past the bar through the back door, and into the back room. It was the sum total of their total worth. The good old boys at the bar hardly turned a head as this little beleaguered parade of three passed behind them. This shabby tavern was now home for the "little man

The first night in the back room of the tavern was a child's nightmare. Still barefoot and dirty I was lifted into the top drawer of the dresser just under the single window. My mother kissed me good night and went back thru the open door into the bar. It was summer, hot and humid. For me the small window, open and just above my head in the top drawer of the squeaky chest of drawers, was a blessing and a curse. It was a relief from the stinky smell of stale beer and cigarette smoke, but it was an open door to the mosquitoes that bit and mercilessly torture me throughout the night. With my small arm I reached out through the opening and felt the rough edge of the broken screen. I tried to cover myself with the scant blankets. The close and constant buzzing followed even under the cloth. There was no escape Mother and Hugo had long since closed the curtain and left for their duties at the bar and I was alone.

During the night, the soon to be regulars in the tavern had arrived in force. It was a loud event with enormous amounts of beer consumed. The revelry in song to "Roll out the Barrel" got louder and louder with each repetition. It still haunts my mind. Even with the raucous tavern sounds, sleep finally claimed me.

For me the small window, open and just above my head in the top drawer of the chest of drawers, was a blessing and a curse. I had swatted until sleep overcame my body and mind. The close and constant buzzing followed even under the cloth. There was no escape. Throughout the night, mosquitoes fed on any exposed skin. I tried to cover myself with the blankets. The first night in the Whalen Tavern was pure hell. It seemed that that opening night went on forever and between the noise and the mosquitoes it was as if the torture would never end.

It was dark in the early morning when Hugo and mother came into the back room, now home, closed the curtain, reached to the light bulb hanging from the ceiling and with a click the light was off. The deep loud sounds of sleep came from the two sleeping on the dirty old mattress on the filthy floor. I did not, or would not bother them.

The early morning sunlight shining in the small window slowly awakened me. I did not know where I was, who I was, or who I was with, so I just curled up tight and tried to not to become an annoyance to them. I would survive. Though I knew not why, I questioned the value of being alive. Frankly I was just hanging on, and though I had to go to the bathroom, I said nothing. It was really uncomfortable. I dared not cry, not knowing what punishment might follow.

I was suddenly scared. It was just last night when my mother, Hugo and I moved into the new abode. With dawn the dim light grew brighter but I could not open my eyes. The early morning sunlight came through my small and screenless window I do not know when the mosquitoes finished their feeding frenzy, but I could feel the welts all over my exposed face and arms. I could not open my eyes except for a narrow squint. I was sure I was blind. I felt panic! I was still in the top drawer of the large old dresser and it was a long way to the floor. I did not know what bladder was, but I knew something was full and I needed relief. Mother stirred, shook her head, stood up and tried to acquaint herself with the surroundings. She moved through the open door to the tavern, must have relieved herself first and returned. She lifted me down and commanded "Follow me." Once inside the tavern she pointed to the open door to the tiny room housing a toilet and a sink. The smell was overpowering. I was barefoot and the wet and sticky urine covered floor was both slippery and tacky, but the overwhelming urge was utmost. It had been a long night.

After relieving myself, I made my way into the back room, every step sticking to the floor. My eyes were still mostly swollen shut. Mother had once again fallen asleep on the filthy mattress on the floor beside Hugo. He had not stirred and the only sign of life was the gasps for air between snores. I was hungry and thirsty.

Only now can I attest to the fact that a feeling came over me. Anger! I was beginning to grasp the depth of my unimportance in their lives. Total discomfort filled every cell in my body and there was nothing I could do about it. What did I do to deserve this? I did not know what it meant, but survival was the key. I would not cry though I did not know why. I had to be tough to make it and could not count on help from anyone. There was no place to go for comfort.

Hungry and thirsty, I sat down on an old blue and white stripped pillow in a corner of the room and curled into a fetal position overwhelmed and scared. I hardly knew my mother.

There had not been any true bonding. No stability just constant moving from place to place

The past had no meaning for me except that everything was constantly different. From day one, it was just hang on, and it was survival day by day. In our society it was not a time of child endangerment concerns.

Life in the tavern became my whole world. The tavern was mostly patronized by men middle aged or older and I was treated as kind of a tavern mascot. The men drank a lot, sang and laughed and seemed to enjoy their life. They had no expectations of anything better. Hugo was seldom present and my mother was the barkeep. She expected no more than beer and cigarettes from life and was satisfied. As long as smoke curled upward from her hand or mouth she seemed pacified.

"Alice! Another round!" was the cry from the booth.

She delivered the libation of choice and gathered the cost for the cash register.

The west side of the building was lined with six booths and the east wall was occupied with the long bar, complete with a brass foot rail and barstools. The north front wall had two large windows with a swinging door in the middle. It was on the south end that a small room, certainly not a bathroom, but a place for excretion existed. Straight south was the torn and dirty curtain to the backroom, my home. The floor had not been cleaned since the time when it was the bank. That was when clean people, walked in and out doing their banking. Today there was no bank in the town. Only the post office is still in operation just west of the tavern. There had been a change in the village and it was economically negative.

In the tavern the good old boys, bib overalls not washed for great lengths of time, shared their chips and strips of dried meat or whatever they had with me as I passed by. Sunday was a problem. God must have said thou shall not drink on Sunday, however, that meant no treats from the bar.

There were times when there was no food so my mom would contact someone they knew and we went to a house for a meal. It was Norwegian food and that probably kept us alive. Today the words haunt me, Rumagrout or something like that, but it filled the void. It is kind of a cream of wheat with no flavor. Krub or klub was another lifesaver. It was made by butchering an animal and the blood was caught in a container as it flowed from the animals neck and then it was mixed and kneaded with flour into softball sized clumps. The clumps were opened and filled with chunks of pork fat and all was dropped into boiling water. When the parcel floated to the surface of the boiling water it was traditionally scooped from the bubbling water with a large wooden spoon. The large clumps of coagulated blood and flour, dark brown in color were dispensed one at a time to each waiting plate. It was not filet mignon, but nobody knew the difference. It filled the fundus.

The total bar room was dark from ceiling to floor with the exception of a few fluorescent signs, colorful, stating the varieties of beer available. Heavy smoke permeated wall to wall and floor to ceiling. For those present, it was a way of life, a comfort zone. It was a tiny town. Everyone knew everyone, where everyone lived, where they worked if they indeed had a job and their family history for several generations. It was an area of a small gene pool. Inbreeding of family lines was the norm. Everybody was related with facial and body types so similar. The apple had not fallen far from the tree.

Chapter 12

Deal! Little Man!

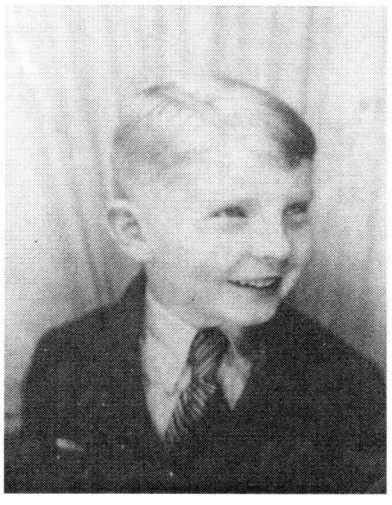

Little Man (Holle Family collection)

"Little man! Come here. Just come up here. It is time you learned to play poker."

There were two men seated on one side of the booth and one on the other. I crawled up into the empty seat, surprised and pleased that someone recognized me as a person. The three scruffy unwashed old men were tipping their glasses of beer with a toast of, "skoal" to each turn of the card.

Soon the dealer said, "Son, it is time for you to learn the game".

I had no idea what the word "game" meant. There they were the three grizzled, cruddy, working men and one little man. The dealer began shuffling the dirty, stained and wrinkled well-used cards. The cards were dealt.....there they were, five cards in front of me on the table. I had my hand, my first hand. I watched as the men cautiously glanced at the cards they were dealt. They tried to hide their delight or disappointment with a poker face. Poker was my first lesson in mathematics and psychology in that tavern.

"Deal!" one of the men said and I dealt the cards.

At age four, I knew nothing and nobody. Everything was new and different. I was not related. Survival was pretty much the order of every the day, but in the booth, seated on the left near the wall, with the three unwashed old men in the other three seats, I began to learn a bit of life. These were people that lived from day-to-day, from beer to beer and cigarette-to-cigarette. They were at the end of the line. Evil no! They just had no hope, only life to the end.

Rap Poker was the name of the game. The glasses of beer were delivered from the bar by Alice one after another. The three poker partner's voices gradually grew louder. The small change bet on each hand seemed to be important. They were quite drunk, but without anger. Each hand ended with a player rapping his knuckles on the table and declaring victory, thus the name "Rap Poker". Soon it was apparent to me that four aces was the hand to achieve. My three fellow players made sure that the cards kept being dealt often ended with all aces in my hand. When this happened to me there was three pair of eyes staring.

"Your turn." the voice commanded.

I tipped up the cards as I had watched the others do. Four aces. They had taught me the value. Undoubtedly they had also staged the result.

At such an early age I was beginning to learn the game, the game of life from the kind old codgers that had taken me under their wings. And so it was that I became a poker player at the age of four in Whalen, Minnesota and the game went on.

"Deal!" I stated in my high child voice.

The three men carefully guarded their cards and so did I. The glances went from eye to eye. Each of them had and used different facial expressions. Each vocally expressed their statements of their hands with bluffing remarks. I listened. I learned. I began to learn the psychology of the game. The bluff. It was not what someone had in their hand, but what they wanted everyone to believe. Soon, a player would rap on the table and everyone showed the cards. I began to learn value. The best part though was four aces. When the deal rotated again to me there was those three pair of eyes staring at me. Again about every forth hand, I would turn over four aces. The worst hand had to buy a drink. I never had to buy.

The loser would call out, "Set'em up!"

Alice would soon appear with a tray, three glasses with foam at the brim and one small glass of soda. I had more sodas than my small body could handle.

I began to understand the life and no longer had any fear. I began to like the tavern life. The glasses of beer kept being delivered from the bar by my mother one after another. They all seemed happy when they were drinking. I never had a bad experience with those people. Today I wonder what has changed. Those people, those men all winners, and sadly they are all gone.

I still remember my first math and psychology lessons from my poker partners in the tavern and my thanks to them. All in! Those were fun times.

Life in the tavern was loose. I have never recovered. Discipline? I had no idea what that meant. Lack of discipline had its root that would plague me for the rest of my life. My wife of 56 years says she married a wild man, so I am! I have no discipline.

Chapter 13

Another Education

Whalan School (courtesy of the Whalan Museum)

The one room school high on the hill with the bell tower still stands much as it did, through many generations. The condition of the building is somewhat better since it has been converted into a single family home and shows pride of ownership. It is a picture for the mind of anyone that questions what life was like in the gentle past. It had a school marm in charge and responsible for the education and safe keep of the children in grades kindergarten through six. In autumn she raked leaves. Winters meant her being there early, sweep the floor and start the fire in the potbellied stove to take the chill off before the children arrived. God bless her! She did not belong to the teachers union. I wish I could recall more about the teacher. She deserves more respect in memory. She always looked the same, and was a comfort. It was something a child could count on every day. Those comforts were few.

I wonder how at four I found my way out the front door of the tavern and up the hill because no one ever took me. My mom had pointed to the building on the hill. It was the typical one room school with the bell tower. It was September, Autumn. I just arrived at the front door, the teacher had no idea who I was, and did I belong to someone? I was assigned a seat and desk on the right side of the room, fourth from the front. After all these decades I could point to that spot on the floor that was my desk. It has been a long way from there to the Universities that have been a big part of my life

I do recall the natural beauty; the Oaks and Maples were in full color in autumn. Halloween came in the small town and they held events for young and old. The oldest of the population gathered in small groups, parties where all were acquainted, they really knew each other and knew what to expect at a Halloween party. This was my first Halloween Party ever. Aside from much consumption of beer and some whiskey most of the revelry was harmless. A large keg of beer was always the centerpiece of the celebration and would be totally consumed before night's end. Songs like 'Roll out the Barrel' filled the night and a good time was had by all.

Whalen had and still has a small town population about 68and within a week I pretty much knew where everything was located and could find my way about by myself. I knew where Chiglo's Ice Cream Shop was and Pete Chiglo was a terrific person. We all headed to his store after school. He gave us ice cream and we looked forward to that delight.

At night sometimes there was a free outdoor movie on the side lawn of the grange building that is now the Whalan Museum. The Haunted House was my first movie. It was quite dark when I told my mother where I was going and left the tavern walking the short block to the grange hall.

I found a seat in the front row of benches and it was just a short time before the creepy film began. It was over in about an hour and the audience rapidly disappeared. The night was very dark. The one block walk back to the tavern seemed much longer in the dark after the scary movie and I jumped and shivered at the slightest sound in the bushes. Soon, with great relief, I approached the front of the tavern. The lighted front windows and the open door with the sound of the music were a great relief. Neither my mom nor Hugo noticed as I passed through the crowd from the front door to the rear. Nobody seemed to care. It was easy to push the curtain aside and go into the safe haven of the back room. Climbing into the top drawer of the chest was difficult but was finally accomplished. The noise from the tavern was comforting. I felt alone but soon fell asleep.

This was the first time in my life that Christmas was celebrated. In the tavern in Whalen there was a tree with decorations, though I knew nothing of the significance or importance of that time of year.

Chapter 14

The Northwestern Hotel

Just when life seemed settled it was time to move again. The move from Whalen happened suddenly.

The old white rusty Ford pulled slowly into the dirt driveway, guided by the two deep ruts with a center row of weeds that scratched the bottom of the car. Where were we now? In the past few months, home had been in the back room of the tavern in tiny Whalen where I began school in kindergarten at four years of age. I do not remember how long that lasted, some months, maybe. A couple of other moves followed. Home in the early years of my life was transient. The usual permanent location of home in the normal American family was something I was never to experience. The next home I remember would be the Northwestern Hotel in Rushford.

A SEED NOT WATERED

Northwestern Hotel (courtesy of Rushford Area Historical Society)

The Northwest Hotel is a thing of the past, alive only in the minds of a few and then only to those that have a memory of a personal experience. So it was, and is with me. Somewhere about the age of four or five, my home was relocated from Whalen to a room on the third floor of the tallest building in Rushford. For me it was a step up! There was a bathroom on every floor! There was running water! I never had a real bath during the time in Whalen, now there was a sink to splash water on my face and a place to bathe. Most of all, there was a little cleaner toilet where one could excrete. At an early age I had learned to just hold it and now a bathroom with plumbing was an absolute luxury. Life was good. The room was below modern standards, but the three of us, my mother, Hugo, and I never expected more or better. It was part of the deal. I was too young to make a judgment, but for me it seemed like a big step in the right direction.

Now, again I had that feeling…..I knew I wanted to be rich.

My mom and Hugo were, as usual, bartenders in the tavern on the first floor. They received a room, some salary and some meals in the small restaurant which was also located on the first floor.

Now, after all these years, I know they also got all the booze and smokes they required on a daily basis, as a perk. It was all part of the deal.

My childhood was constantly clouded in the smoke of Old Gold cigarettes. It was the smoke of their life on a daily schedule and mine by virtue of the constant cloud.

In those days, traveling salesmen plied their goods to local businesses. The lobby as one entered the front glass door of the hotel, was rather dingy, dull, dark and dank. Many large leather chairs furnished the room and were almost always filled with men smoking cigars and chewing tobacco. Numerous spittoons located at critical areas caught most of the expectoration and the rest became part of the stain and odor that gave the Northwest Hotel its identity. It was a comfort zone for those that had this stopover in their territory.

For me it was lonely and scary. Saturday night was the worst, I was always alone in the dark on the third floor but on Saturday night the noise from the tavern below was not as warm as the Whalan Tavern sounds and it made sleep impossible. Besides that the pungent cigarette smoke was everywhere. One such evening, the revelry was overwhelming. I slid off the cot and made my way toward the light in the cracks around the edge of the door. The squeaking sound made me catch my breath. I peeked into the long hall hoping no one was there and then made my way to the stairs following the sound of the noise. My pajamas did not fit and kept slipping down. Holding the waistband I turned right at the bottom of the stairs. The room was filled with people drunk and beyond. I must have tickled their fancy as they broke into raucous laughter. I knew embarrassment. After all these years I remember that sound.

I moved forward between the rows of booths clutching my pajamas. There it was….the bar! There was my mother! The crowd was lined up at the bar and she was dispensing the booze as fast as she could. She did not notice as I peeked around the end of the bar. It was not her fault because Saturday night was packed with patrons. I turned, made my way back between the rows of booths and made the turn up that large wooden stairs to the room called home.

Now…… I was becoming aware of my status.

I started in the first grade at the Rushford School while living in the room on the third floor of the Northwestern Hotel and school was just a short walk away. School was never an important issue to mother and Hugo and that was to follow me through high school.

Chapter 15

What Delight! What pain.

I found myself looking at an unfamiliar room. We had moved again. The move from the Northwestern Hotel room to a small one room apartment in Rushford was probably done in one hour or less. I was sitting on the corner of a couch in a strange place by myself when one morning Hugo and my mother entered the door and I knew something was going to happen. Hugo's hands were held behind his back and I could hear small sounds. Out came his hand and there it was, the puppy. My puppy! It crawled on my lap, wriggled, turned over and over and I'm sure that its smile was as big as mine. We were meant for each other. That little dog could not get close enough to me. He curled up under my chin and we fell asleep. Throughout the night I put my hand on its warm little back. We were pals, we needed each other.

I awoke to "Damn! Damn dog!" The loud voice was filled with anger.

I reached for my puppy. It was not there. Hugo was sweeping under the couch with a broom. Soon a whimper and the little guy rolled over and over out from the hiding place. Hugo held the pup in one hand and angrily rubbed the slippers into the puppy's face. The poor little dog's eyes told of his fright. Hugo stormed in rage out with the little critter in hand, and that was the last I saw of my puppy.

After that terrible disappointment I experienced an unexpected treat from my grandfather Albert, Lloyd Humble, who I called Uncle Lloyd and another uncle. This trio surprised me one day by picking me up as I sat on the back porch of my grandfather's house with not much to do and they took me to a baseball game in Lanesboro, Minnesota. You can't imagine my delight. Lanesboro was like going to the other side of the world to me since I had never been there. It was an 18 mile trip from Rushford but I didn't mind because I was sitting in the car with these three men who thought I was important enough to include in the trip to the ballgame. I felt very important and pleased. I am sure I smiled all day.

House on Mill Street (courtesy of Rushford Area Historical Society)

When we returned I was told that we were moving to the house on Mill Street. I really didn't know why but I detected that Hugo and mom were happy about finding a place.

In a short time this had been a very gypsy life. I was still in the first grade and the house was only a block from school.

Hugo and mom rented the whole first floor apartment of the old two story house owned by a very nice spinster.

The dream of the American family with a home was far from reality. But this was more like living in a house not a room even if it was rented. In my mother's life, she never lived in a house that was not rented.

Thus far, in the last three years, we lived in the back room of the Whalan Tavern, a room on the third floor of the Rushford's Northwestern Hotel, in a small back single room somewhere in town, and now on the ground floor of an old house made into an apartment. The new abode was the bottom floor of a house owned by a very nice lady who came from a small town to the south called Mabel.

The only problem I remember was that the only bathroom was upstairs and other people lived up there and everyone shared the bathroom.

To the south in the next lot was a gas station and one day I was told to go get a can of kerosene. Without question I headed for the station just two doors away.

The man took the rusty can in hand and began to fill the container. "Do you have the money?" he asked, but he knew I was sent without any. I began to learn shame. The man scribbled on a small pad, handed the gas can to me and said, "Give this to your mother. God bless." I saw the kindness in his face and eyes and I like him regardless of my shame.

This man and his wife, two really nice people brought a bright spot into my life. They lived in the second story apartment directly across the street from his gas station. They expected little, but were truly happy with the small things in a simple life. Somehow, somewhere, they found a match for their little female black and white Boston terrier. The mating produced two puppies. The man had searched the funnies for appropriate names and came up with Maggie and Jiggs, two of the popular comic figures in the newspapers of the day. They had no children and they kindly took me under their wing. Soon after the pups birth, it is the custom to dock the tails of Boston Terriers, but these kind hearted folks did not have the heart to do it, and the pups kept the typical hairless screw tail that resembled small bolts of lightning.

The adjoining building was a one story structure with a flat roof, housing one of the three dental offices in the town. The flat roof became the outdoor area for the mother dog and the two pups. Ultimately, the noise of the play above the patients in the dentist's chair dictated change.

Chapter 16

Jiggs

One day that kind man who owned the gas station in Rushford and lived across the street appeared at my door with a puppy in each hand. I stood in the open door as high as his belt buckle. He just stood there and held them out and I could tell he wanted me to pick one. How could anyone pick just one? I had a feeling he knew of the fate of my first puppy.

I stared at them. I knew it would be my good luck if I could have one. They were both perfect in my eyes and I said, "I'll take this one!"

Jiggs and Richard (Holle Family collection)

The little pup in my left hand squirmed, the tiny tongue licking my hand. But, it was the eyes that melted my soul. Jiggs. I had chosen Jiggs, the male. This time I was determined to not let anything happen to this puppy. Hugo would have to run over me first!

The little black and white puppy had perfect colors and markings and looked to me like a show dog, except for the tail. The tail, the screw tail looked like a six inch lightning bolt, bare and bent in the middle. He had worn most of the tail hair off except for a tuft at the end. Jiggs may not have been perfect, but he was perfect for me!

His diet consisted of whatever was available and sometimes this created a problem. Jiggs ate anything and as a result produced large quantities of gas. Sometimes acquaintances of

Hugo and my mom would stop by to drink beer. Jiggs was not a shy dog and he liked company. He would quietly lay down close by the chair of a guest. That is when it always happened. The expressions on the faces told the story. Guests looked up with raised eyebrows seeming to say without words, *it wasn't me*. Jiggs became a legend for his hospitality. I think everyone in town knew of my puppy.

Now, I tell you, loud noises drove Jiggs crazy. The local fire station was only 200 feet from the front door on the opposite side of the street. Whenever the siren sounded Jiggs would howl loud enough to wake the dead. In the summer, Jiggs would burst through the screen door and wildly chase the fire truck. The screen didn't have a chance but we fixed it once..

Frequently the driver of the fire engine could not see the tiny black and white terror biting at the tires of the fire truck as if on a mission to kill it. Jiggs would come limping home. He led a blessed life and generally recovered as good as new. We finally didn't bother to fix the screen on the door.

Snore! Jiggs was a master of this. He would lay by the back door like a good watchdog and in his sleep he snored loudly. Finally I tied a string around the bend in his screw tail and the other end was attached to my bed. When the snoring made sleep impossible I would give the string a gentle tug and everyone could go back to sleep. Life with Jiggs was interesting.

Besides the owner of the gas station there were other businesses close by. There was the shoemaker who had a shoe repair business in the front twenty feet of the next building. Shoemaker was a misnomer, he repaired shoes, not produced them. To say it was a modest business is an understatement. As one entered the front door, the first thing to catch attention was the smell, the odor of old leather, old shoes that were being fixed for another chance at life. A large shelf system filled the back wall. Each level was filled with pairs of shoes neatly stacked side by side with small white tags indicating ownership. It was a great mixture of ladies shoes of various color and style, and children's tiny varieties all mixed with conservative masculine types. He always knew each and every shoe, in what state of repair, who was the owner by first name and everyone in the family.

Many years later as I stood there after the notorious Rushford flood, facing that now silent storefront I glanced down at the toes of my $100. shoes that I was about to dispose of in the next trash collection. The kind man would have done minor repairs, polished, and given me a bill for the price of a cup of coffee. Those people were of a different time. They did not live 'high on the hog'. They 'made do', I well remember those words. They were kind good people.

Even though I had contact with these remarkable people, I never fit. I could not, would not fit. It was not my life. Here was that feeling again,....I didn't know what I wanted to do, but I sure as hell knew what I did not want to do!

Now I do an about face and look at the stark grey stucco front of the Legion Hall of my memory. It had obviously been closed for many years. Mom and Hugo belonged to the legion because mom had a brother that was killed in the war so she and Hugo were eligible to belong and this soon became their hideaway. Hugo had flat feet and was therefore able to dodge the obligation of service. Soon the pair had a new job as bartenders in the basement tavern of the Legion Hall, a vocation of which they had considerable experience. Living directly across the street made getting to work on time easy for them. And for me I would sneak down the stairway, peer around the corner at the bottom of the stairs and see them serving the endless beers to the full bar. I could sneak into the back room and play on the beer cases. I came out of there after hours of play covered with dust and dirt. I very seldom had a bath and when I did it was just a sponge bath which only seemed to spread the mud on me. I stayed dirty day and night.

I would run up the stairs before anyone knew I was there, run across the street and in the front door of our house where my pal Jiggs was always waiting. No one knew I had been there or cared.

Chapter 17

Embarrassing Moments

As I mentioned, at the new place we lived the bathroom was upstairs. Everyone in the building shared the one bathroom. One day shortly after we moved in a lady walked in and went to the bathroom right next to me when I was in the tub. That was the first and last bath I had in the tub. After that I did sponge baths in the kitchen sink. I never got fully clean until I got into high school and took my first shower it was the first one ever. That was the best thing about school.

In those days bathroom conveniences were not abundant and people had a "Thunder Mug" under the bed which they used to go to the bathroom in at night. One night I went into my mother and Hugo's room to use the "Thunder Mug" and they were having sex. I closed the door and I never used the "Thunder Mug" again. So what did I do?...... I whizzed out the window through the screen, such as it was. In the winter it froze on the screen and you couldn't see through it. The snow outside had yellow spots until spring.

On the brighter side we had a telephone with a crank on the side and after turning the crank 'central' answered "Yes, Richard?" I requested to talk to Dave and I was connected without a telephone number or last name....she just knew.

At eight I was active, and wanting to do something. It was summer vacation. The weather was hot and very humid. For me being bored was never, nor is it now an excusable state of mind. I thought very early I am not bored, but rather that I am boring. This is a tough assignment for a young man. I asked my Mom, what I could do even though I knew she did not want to be bothered and I found out very soon that I should not have asked.

She sat with her legs spread over the arms of the chair with the fan blowing directly to her body and said, "I am on my last cigarette," as the smoke curled out of her nostrils, "go to the store and get a pack of Old Gold and put it on the bill".

The store was but a block away. It had been my grandfather's market that he sold when his son, my father died. I was on a mission to request credit for cigarettes at the age of eight for mom's nicotine habit. My eyes were just high enough to see over the counter. The lady at the check stand scowled when I asked for the cigarettes. I was too young to know of cigarettes. I only knew the house I called home was constantly filled with smoke from morning to night from those things. To me, this was normal and I thought people needed cigarettes as much as food.

The woman summoned a man from the rear of the store. He too was very unpleasant. Looking over his glasses, he said you cannot buy cigarettes. I did not know I was too young. I was scared out of my wits and did not know I was doing something wrong.

"Mom said to get a pack of Old Gold and put it on the bill." I explained.

In and angry voice he sternly stated, "You go home right now. Tell your mother to come and buy her own cigarettes and tell her to pay her bill before she can buy anything in this store!"

His anger frightened me. I did not know anything about bills, but there was something wrong and I felt awful. I was learning about life.

Chapter 18

Sunday and Bootlegging

It was a lifetime of hate for Sunday, every Sunday. It was a day of structure, consistent order unlike the other days of each week. It seemed that the sky was always dreary and grey on Sunday. The alarm would promptly ring at seven and call me to my duty at church.

"Onward Christian Soldiers......" We all sang with gusto as the service was ending and the Sunday procession was getting ready to slowly exit toward the two great entryways of the magnificent limestone structure. "....marching as to war!" rang, out as the portals slowly opened. It was probably my favorite of the congregation's every Sunday attempts at music. Throughout the proceedings the pastor would announce and command the flock, the sheep, to turn to page such and such of the Hymnal and sing praise to God as the organ played. To me church music was and is the most boring and unmusical droning noise that one can imagine. Throughout the congregation, no two voices were ever on the same note and the least musically talented always bellowed with the greatest volume. At least Onward Christian Soldiers has a melody line that almost everyone can at least hum.

Christian teachings had been a bulwark in my early life. It dictated the difference between right and wrong. The awakening was gradual and not without discomfort, actually painful. Blind obedience? It is no doubt a source of many of the serious problems in society today. Do not question! Obey without question!

The second line, "marching as to war!" Kill? Why? What would Jesus say? Kill? I don't think so, or the concept of Jesus is not that I was taught as a child. Thou shall not kill!

As the faithful filed through the right or left portal just as their parents and grandparents and in some cases the great grandparents, immigrants from the old country did. The word stability seemed to fit. Generations came and went and were venerated.

The bell tolled. We, the now enlightened, emerged into the sunlight, either on the right or left as was the structured custom. Once outside, in front, handshakes and greetings were exchanged. While families were going home to chicken dinner I was headed to my other responsibility on the Lord's Day and I was only eight years old.

Chapter 19

Gottabottle?

There it was...... the knock on the back door. Tap, tap and tap. As I had been instructed, I was waiting, seated at the chrome and red table.

"When someone knocks, peek out the door," was Hugo's command. "Tell him it is six dollars."

I understood. I had had early math lesson playing poker. Six dollars for one bottle of Four Roses Whiskey was the going price. I was eight years old and acquainted with numbers. Honor thy father and mother had been ingrained in my mind and I had to obey as directed. Though my father had died years previously, I knew I must do as the man that my mother married ordered, as though he were my dad. It was supposed to be the right thing to do so I opened the door just a crack and peered out.

"Gotabottle?" The man asked.

There he was, a very slight disheveled man and he opened his mouth in a toothless grin. His unshaved face and dirty clothing was a scary apparition. One eye starred directly at my face. The other eye wandered aimlessly around, never finding focus. Now I understood why everyone calls him cockeyed Ole and he scared the hell out of me.

"Six dollars." was my request.

The man reached his hand into the opening and passed some dollar bills into the waiting hand. I closed the door, counted the money, the six one dollar bills, and hid them in the secret drawer in the pantry. Then, the next step was to go to the closet in their bedroom, which was the hiding place for the illegal whiskey. There they were the two cases of Four Roses Whiskey, a local favorite. The lid of the top case was open. I reached into the box and grabbed the neck of the first bottle and returned to the back door. Cautiously, I opened the door and saw that my first client was still waiting. Passing the bottle into the anxiously awaiting hand I heard the church bells chiming.

The man gave me a toothless grin; it was my mother's father, my maternal grandfather. The man probably did not know there was any relationship and I was not about to inform him. Then, bottle in hand, the creature disappeared. He was on his way to the 'Hell Hole' where the old men did their drinking and passed the bottle. They hid away from all others.

I was alone again. Though I had no idea where they were, my mother and Hugo said they would return. It was Sunday and I knew they were not in church.

Chapter 20

Rent was 25cents a week.

There was another great and kind man that owned and operated a bicycle repair shop in an old building next to the Masonic Temple. He was somewhat tall, slender and kind. My old red and white radio flyer bicycle frequently needed tire repair, and I really needed the bike for my new paper route. When I stopped at The Bicycle Shop to pick up my bike I would ask, "How much?"

He would just slowly and gently shake his head and say, "No".

Friday! The weekend and school was out. My first job started the next day. I was eleven going on twelve and now I had a paper route. The Minneapolis Star Tribune was my first employer. It was a responsibility and I appreciated the opportunity. Every morning, a wired bundle of newspapers was dropped on the corner of Jesse and Mill Streets. I delighted in clipping the wire, stuffing the newspapers in my paper sack and starting delivery before dawn. It gave a feeling of personal achievement, doing something of value. The paper had to be delivered regardless of the season or daily weather. There were times, many times when I wondered if it was worth the effort. Those thoughts were forgotten when on Saturdays the collections for the newspaper subscriptions were made. I paid the Tribune and I received my wages. Weekly netting $1.25 on a paper route I began to learn economic independence at that age. It was a seven-days a week job. The paper sack was full as the bicycle and I peddled off into the early hours on our mission. The season and the weather always had a part in the daily journey. At this age, I learned that Minnesota winters were bad.

Then, one day in the late morning I learned another lesson. Soon after I began collecting for the paper Hugo said, "It is time we have a little talk. Your mother and I must pay rent and buy groceries, so it is time for you to start paying your way. You earn $1.25 per week. It is time for you to pay a quarter each week for room and board."

It was not much, but I began to learn that I had to pay my way. I thought all kids in my class probably paid their own way. Hugo, they called him Hooks, never had a job except behind the bar.

Early I learned about deadbeats, some people just do not pay their bills. Sometimes I had to make up the difference out of my wages if they could not pay.

Every Saturday I delivered the morning papers, later repeated my steps, knocking on the doors to collect. Nobody taught me a good approach.

In retrospect after all these decades, I remember the excuses. The, "Well, I just don't have it now," routine."

When it was time for the bottom line, though, I had to pay for the newspapers every week and then pay a quarter for rent when I got back to the house, I could never use an excuse like "I just don't have it now." If there were money after the week's bills, I saved as much as possible just in case I wouldn't have enough for the next week's bills. Throughout the week I would revisit the doors of the deadbeats that had not paid. Whether they paid or not, I learned that I had to pay the paper and my room and board.

I still to this day cannot call where I lived 'home'. It was like a boarding house. I never spoke with my peers about their homes. I just assumed everyone lived the same.

My friends and I were spreading our wings at this age and we enjoyed ice skating to the little town of Peterson three miles away on the Root River. We had money for a cup of hot chocolate and then we skated back to Rushford. We skied on the small ski jump in town. We fished and hunted together. We climbed the bluffs in the area and explored everything around our town. We were altar boys at church and sang in the choir. I spent as much time as I could with them and they made me feel comfortable. These were my family.

Chapter 21

Noodles and Cupcakes

The farm kids had lunch at school but the city kids had to go home. It was but a block for me to walk from school to where I lived for my lunch. Everyday Jiggs was at the front door, tail waging and head whirling to see his pal home at last. I slowly opened the front door and peered into the front room. Mom sat askew in a chair, listening to the soap opera of the time. Smoke from her Old Gold curled upward from her nose.

While eating my noodles I happened to say to her, "You shouldn't drink so much."

I didn't see it coming. Her hand hit the side of my head. I was stunned. My elbow landed on the edge of the dish of boiled macaroni which flipped throwing the noodles into the air. The noodles were scattered all over. They were wet and rather slimy. The front of my shirt was covered with noodle juice.

Mom screamed, "Clean up your mess!"

I could not allow myself to cry, it was not manly, but tears ran down my cheeks, "I want to run away." I squeaked.

"There is the door you little bastard." she said as she pointed and gestured to the back door. "Take that damned dog with you!" she shouted pointing at little Jiggs cowering close to the door on the rag rug.

The pooch had no idea of the situation, only of the rage from my mom. There was no eye contact between mother and son. She lit up another Old Gold and disappeared into the front room. I left that day in spirit. Every Sunday I was taught to love and honor his mother, but all I could feel was fear and hate. From that day forth I was never able to erase those feelings so deeply planted in my soul and I never ever got over the regret of being born. I never wanted to be a bother for anyone. Even with zero self-esteem I survived one day at a time, though my hold on life was always slim and without question of its value or when and where to check out.

It was hard to think. I scrapped up the macaroni as best I could and placed it in the garbage bag in the corner. I was a mess, but the bell was ringing and it was time for social studies. Silence was the only way to describe my entrance. All eyes were on the shirt covered with the remains of lunch. It had to be hard not to laugh and giggle as my classmates watched me enter. The teacher only raised his eyes as I made my way to my seat. He undoubtedly knew something unpleasant had occurred during the lunch break and thus did no inquire about my tardy entrance.

The silence of the classroom gave time to think and my thoughts went back to the little black and white dog, my small friend that never meant harm to anyone. It was impossible to think of early exploration and war. I only hoped Jiggs would be there and safe when I returned.

I promised myself, *Soon I would make a change*, and I did.

For me, the next day was the day of emancipation. I walked past the opening in the huge hedge that opened to the house of despair. I had the pocket change that gave me the guts to strike out on my own. I ran to the café to order lunch instead of stopping at home. I could now pay my own way. I went to Niggle's Café.

Niggle's Café was where an incident occurred during a night of drinking between a classmate if my father and my mother. She claimed he called her a whore. She slapped his face. She threatened to sue him. She was always going to sue someone. I did not know the meaning of sue or whore. The town folks seemed to hear about the event on the gossip train that ran around the small town. That event stamped me for life. Soon I was dumped in the trash can at school by some large boys and called names. I never had the experience of what people describe as normal family life like they did. I was growing up and growing aware. In retrospect, I have wondered if the allegations had any basis. But now I just don't give a damn.

Niggle's Café (courtesy of Rushford Area Historical Society)

Niggle's Café was owned and run by Ben Niggle. He was a well-respected and admired man in Rushford. Ben was a true champion who never missed a school ball game. He was a great supporter of the town teams. You could rely on seeing him at all the home or away games. I don't think he ever missed one. The café was full of adults for the noon meal. I moved through the space between the occupied booths and the bar area. The patrons were polite and allowed this child to pass through to the rear of the café. There were more booths on the left and a lunch counter on the right.

One man behind the counter had worked at the cafe for many years and he asked, "What would you like?" As I sat at the lunch counter I ordered Tomato Soup and crackers and from then on he always knew the answer.

Everyday midway down the middle of the cafe this same person spotted me. He was an adult that kids seldom but occasionally has the good luck to meet. Campbell's Tomato Soup was the soup d'jour every day. I was always offered extra crackers that were gratefully dunked into the tasty broth. Fifteen cents was the bill and I paid it with pride. To this day Campbell's Cream of Tomato soup is my favorite, and I still remember Red giving me extra crackers.

I seldom had any breakfast in my early years and so now on my own each morning I went two doors down to the bakery that Sis Konetchy owned and I ordered chocolate cupcakes. I started going to the bakery every morning and Sis had 4 or 6 chocolate cupcakes ready in a small pink box. Sis was a gentle kind person and mother of a friend. I was basically surviving now on my own with less contact with where I lived.

I would like to feel sorry for my mother's miserable life, but I just can't do it. I feel rage welling up when I think about those formative years. I guess I should forgive and forget. I have tried. Can't. Let God have a shot at that.

Chapter 22

Newspapers and Pharmacy

During a young man's life, he is lucky to meet a fine adult that is a real positive role model. I was fortunate to have two such men in my senior year. Mid-teens found my lifetime friend, a couple of years older, was graduating from high school. My good friend that I have always called Ronnie, and that everyone now knows as Dr. Ron, was going to graduate from our high school. Ron worked at the local pharmacy but his job would be open and he would be off to college. Ron helped me into that job at the local pharmacy. I relished the opportunity.

I felt a new awakening in me. I was trusted by Christy Christenson and became a regular employee. I had keys to open up in the mornings early hours and light the fire in the basement with coal. On Saturdays I shoveled coal to its place in the corner after the delivery down the chute. In the winter I started the fire before going to school. I walked in the snow in the early hours and looked back to see my footprints as I went to my responsibility. I was alone but this feeling was good.

Christy the pharmacist knew I wanted to keep my job at the drug store, but also to play on the football team. One Saturday morning after washing the huge front windows, Christy beckoned me to the table where prescriptions were filled. A plan for work hours and free time for practice and football games was far more than I had ever hoped for and I showed my appreciation by careful diligence in all of my duties. I worked before and after school at Christie's pharmacy. I always thought all kids had some kind of job, earned a wage, chipped in at home and paid their room and board. People spoke of an allowance, but I never knew the meaning and never asked.

The pharmacist was a fine man and a great role model, something I really needed.

No more newspapers! The drug store job provided much more responsibility and trust. That was a period when I grew, not only in size, but more importantly, character!

I more than doubled my income to $5.17 per week. Of course this meant it was time for another little talk. The ante for room and board was raised. Every Friday I gave the expected amount to my mother. As long as I had a job, be it the paper route or at the drug store, all was well; though I never had a feeling of home. It was more than ever like a boarding house.

I had begun to make my way and had had my fill of bad advice. I was not listening to Hugo and mother. No more! Hugo and mother's advice was to have all your teeth pulled, and they never said why. Another was not to ever buy a house because you will be forced to pay taxes. My mother had never lived in her own home. Hooks would not stand for it. He made his way through life without a regular job. They, the two of them, did tend different bars occasionally at various taverns in towns here and there, but none of those positions lasted long. Home had always been a short stay in a room in various places with old mattresses on the floor. To say it was unclean would be an undeserved complement. Bad smells were always present. Sanitary facilities were unknown. I had little contact with others and assumed everyone lived the same.

School and education was another case of bad advice. My mother quit school in the 11th grade and Hooks felt no need to go beyond eighth grade. Just get C's on your report card was their advice, their order to me. That is O. K. What an awful way to destroy a child. I have never recovered. I will not put into print my feelings for those people, one of whom unfortunately, was my mother.

Chapter 23

The Sanctuary

A small one-way street still separates the churches from a narrow block of land in Rushford. The Tew Library fills the easternmost portion of that land. It was donated to the city by the Tew Family and can be seen on the front of this still modest but impressive building. The Tew Library is the only indication of their past presence. The library is a stately conservative brick building having an aura of lasting stability. It is an old building, well built, but also with some areas of treatable obsolescence. It was that family's legacy to Rushford, and indeed was a fine gift. It certainly deserves respect and a bit of reverence.

A small lawn fronts the structure which is setback from the street and during warm seasons the front is decorated with flowerbeds that delight the eye.

As a youth, I used the library. The librarian was an elderly lady that lived but a block away from her work. She, to the best of my knowledge was a spinster whose whole life revolved around the Tew Library. What an incredible asset for Rushford to have a person so dedicated for so many years.

This librarian was certainly in command. There was never noise of any sort within those walls. Her clothing always seemed the same, dark and drab. She was helpful and kind, but she was also stern. Her gentle caring side showed as she would keep new books under the counter and when my friends and I came in she would bring them out especially for us to see first. We felt special. I am not sure I ever saw a smile light up her face. She was the kind of person a kid would like in that position and my friends and I did. She had our respect. Also, in a way, she was kind of scary like someone not needing a costume on Halloween. The library was the only thing she had need of in her life. She has a place in the memory of some of us and the feeling is positive.

The Tew Library certainly has a deep magnetism which is a unique feeling for any and all that have experienced that draw. It has been a personal experience with each of us, almost holy, as one enters and then becomes immersed within those walls of knowledge.

The modest warm structure, St. Joseph's, is only a stone's throw away. Another small one-way street leading in the opposite direction separates the St. Joseph's Catholic Church from the library. St. Josephs is brick, simple, unpretentious and a warm delight to the eye. The brick parish house to the rear of the church matches and complements St. Josephs.

On the other side of the library is the impressive limestone Rushford Lutheran Church. It was built in 1906 of local limestone and seems to reach to heaven. I know it well. Three friends and I were altar boys there most of our young lives. These friends were my family. One of these three friends and I are still very close. To this day, even though we went separate way to opposite ends of the country we still meet yearly. Sadly the other two are not with us anymore.

With the large limestone and stately Rushford School across the street this section of Rushford has been a pivotal neighborhood for generations.

Anyone and everyone growing up in Rushford were stamped in some way by the houses of religion, separated by the domains of knowledge. In addition, Rushford boasts two other fine congregations- Presbyterian and Episcopal- both with their beautiful houses of worship and the faithful in attendance every Sunday morning grace the streets of Rushford. Same God, I guess. Same faith, sort of. Belief in something, maybe, I just never got it. I went through the motions because I thought it was right, but never knew why. Too young and too scared to question, but creating the schism that ultimately drove me away from organized religion and my understanding of the meaning of God. I know there is conflict between the congregations over their different patterns and practices, and I am repulsed by the thought of it.

Now, this is a real conflict. Should the library be demolished in the name of progress? Eliminated for what purpose? Throughout the decades, some very historic buildings in this small town have been leveled in the name of progress. The few buildings that have been constructed on those sites lack character and have no sense of art. There is no doubt that a few individuals have profited from this "process of progress" but at the sacrifice of true historic sites in Rushford. If the past path of progress continues there will no longer be a trace of the history of Rushford. In the future who would be so foolish as to donate anything to the city expecting it would be held in some form of perpetuity?

Chapter 24

You Could Go To Yale!

I can remember my mother's visit to school, on open house night. I was in the fourth grade. That was it! That was the one and only time. In a way I cannot believe that I, a senior citizen, still retain that fact.

Education was not important in the house where I lived. I was instructed to just get C's as that was good enough. I guess they felt that was the height of my ability. Just get C's. I could do that in my sleep and that is what I did. Shame.

My mother had quit school in the 11th grade and had sort of a pride in that accomplishment. She did not finish the 11th grade. Hugo was done in the 8th grade. He didn't think there was anything they could teach him that he did not already know. Frankly, people like that should not be allowed to be in charge of a child's life. They both clearly stated they knew everything.

In retrospect, I was one of the worst students in my class. I never took a book home for homework. I always sat in the back row. I am surprised I reached graduation in high school.

Before graduation and after our final test I was summoned by the superintendent. He greeted me and said, "Richard, you did great on the test, you could go to Yale." I wish now I could have told him that I made it on a National Science Foundation Grant.

I graduated and the graduation ceremony is still in my memory. Pomp and Circumstance. It was a time for family parties. A time for family achievement! Not I. Nobody was in the audience to watch the diploma pass into my hand. I wasn't surprised.

Diploma in hand, it was a short walk to the place where I lived. While my classmates had parties at home, Jiggs and I sat and listened to the radio. I knew they were across the street at the Legion Club Bar and would be home at closing time. I no longer cared.

Chapter 25

Sports and tragedy

It was a beautiful summer day, very warm but not stifling hot. The great American game of baseball was in the air with its small town anticipation. We were the visitors.

A little pepper game before the first inning would soon commence, short to first, to third, second to first, first to short with the constant chatter of camaraderie of those in the infield. The activity stirred up the dust between the bases. The smell of the infield dust has a character of its own and once one has had that experience, it is never forgotten. The bleachers small and rickety were filled with town folks, scruffy people, farmers and a few from the surrounding area. This was a cross section of the local humanity.

The coin toss had decided that the home team; Spring Grove would be first at bat. Our team ran out to the field. Spring Grove was and is a settlement of Norwegian immigrant families like Rushford, closely related from the old country. They are hard workers with pride in the achievements of their families. They were ardent supporters and it showed.

The team was ready. Fired up! The heavy grey wool baseball uniforms of the day were probably the most uncomfortable clothing ever worn by man. Sweat poured from every pore in our bodies. The fabric had a quality that created an itch on every square inch of the torso. Yet, every one of the nine young men on the diamond on that day would not have traded places with anyone.

It was an away game, not a home game, and was the first varsity game that I had a starting assignment. Spring Grove was the home team and the small bleacher section was filled with locals that loved the game while small tots ran around playing their own games. Parents and other relatives turned out to watch hoping to see their relative make it to the 'bigs' and put their town on the map. It was early in the season and expectations were high.

I had played little time in the senior year on the football squad and less minutes on the basketball floor. Baseball was my chance, maybe.

Mom and Hugo had never attended a game in which I played, and now there they were on the far right side of the bleachers, midway back from the front row. They did not have a regular job, so they finally decided to attend a game. I was really surprised but secretly pleased. The smoke curling up from the Old Gold's made it easy to spot them.

I heard my mother shouting "Kill the umpire."

Standing six feet to the left of second base, I tried to catch their attention with a wave, but they were totally engaged in discussion with those around them.

"Batter up!" was the strident command from the umpire behind home base. A cheer went up from the bleachers.

"Batter up was once again the command."

Our little southpaw pitcher was rubbing his left shoulder and furtively glancing over his right shoulder as he was making sure that we in the infield were all in place, poised for action. This was my first inning, the first inning of my life. I did not know if anyone else could hear my knees knocking. I was sweating and nervous.

The first batter strode confidently to the plate, scratched his cleats on the baseball shoes into the ground, raising that baseball dust. All eyes were focused on the batter.

I secured my position about six feet to the left of the second base bag. Hands on my knees was my stance, like I had observed in older players. I waited for play to progress. Here comes the first pitch the wind up and the pitcher threw the ball. The sound of the bat was a loud crack! The ball was rolling toward me at flying speed. Our coach 'Soup' Winblad had coached us to get down on one knee, block the ball with your body, glove the ball and throw it to first base for the out! I stood, bent over, and watched as the ball......... scooted between my legs. Astonishment! The ball rolled behind me into the outfield and I had my first error in baseball.

The runner stood with his right foot firmly and safely on first base. I felt like sinking into the ground. My confident chatter to the pitcher was gone. I glanced at the bleachers. Mom and Hugo were gone. I do not know if it was embarrassment or if it had always been their plan to head for the local tavern. I will never know if they saw the error. No one ever said anything. The second batter took a wild swing at the first pitch. The line drive was screaming over my head. I jumped and reached and felt the ball slam into my glove. The runner from first base was close and I thrust my gloved hand to his back. Did they ever know?

Soup Winblad was a tough football coach, a taskmaster each day on the hot afternoons on the practice field. But finally it was time for the first football game of the season on Friday night. I knew it was a dream that had almost come to an end. It was required that each player have football shoes. After paying room and board, I did not have enough left from my paycheck to buy football shoes and I knew coach had looked the other way every day when I showed up for practice in tennis shoes.

After showering, I gathered my helmet, pads, and gear and said, "Coach, I am turning in my gear. I have not been able to buy my shoes."

Those steel blue eyes focused on me with my head bowed. "Come with me was the sharp command." We stopped in front of the equipment room door. He opened the door slightly, reached his hand around the edge of the door, flipped on the light switch and said "Go find your shoes"!

A few hours later, I lined up at right end when the whistle signaled the start of the game.

This moment was electric in my life, due to a great man Coach Soup Winblad.

Chapter 26

MUD!!!

Einar Erickson was a tough Norwegian with hands the size I had never seen. He was a mason who did concrete and rock work. He was a slight of stature man with a tremendous work ethic. Many of the attractive rock walls in town were constructed by Einar and are still doing their job. He relished picking up large limestone rocks, the bigger the better. All the veins stood out on his forehead as he strained and smiled to be picking up the biggest stone he could find. Einar worked six days a week and I had a job with him for a few summers.

We jacked up large barns on local farms. You could hear the barn creak and groan as it went up just enough to allow us to knock out the rock foundations and replace the rocks with new concrete around them. Ole also worked with Einar while I mixed the concrete or MUD as they called it. When they were ready they shouted, "MUD! MUD!" I was mixing and delivering as fast as I could. Mixing the concrete with water, putting it in the wheelbarrow and delivering it over an uneven board path through the dirt and cow manure were a challenge. For an undernourished thin teenage kid this was back breaking work six days a week and ten hours a day. I was really earning and saving my money. I planned to go to college.

We got paid on Saturday and had Sunday off. Quite often Ole did not make it to work on Monday and when he finally got there he had a hangover and was broke.

Me, I saved my money because I was going to go to college.

Chapter27

Church Conflict

The towering Lutheran Church built in 1906 could be seen from just about anywhere in this small town. It is a magnificent structure, each of the thousands of native limestone blocks were carved one at a time by the hands of local artisans, stone masons that had learned their trade from the generations past. Pride in the craft was exhibited in each of the finished stones. As all great works of art, no two were alike; each stone with its own character built a monument that would last for ages. Standing in front of the church, if one gazed to the east, the quarry could be seen on the southern edge high on the bluff that was the source of all the limestone blocks. The material had been removed by hand, loaded on horse driven carts and hauled down a narrow winding dirt road into the city. Each step of the construction process was wrought with danger. The finished edifice is a true work of art with its stained glass windows recognizing sacrifice of past parishioners which stands as a mark of stability and takes one's breath away.

Throughout my youth, the very appearance of the grand Lutheran Church was at once awe inspiring yet somehow, cold. Many of the parishioners, maybe most, wore a stern face and their conduct was reserved. But it was an environment to which I had to flee to try to find happiness.

Mom and Hooks never attended church of any denomination yet condemned and cursed most of the Christian faiths. I don't really know how I came to be a part of the Lutheran Church every Sunday morning for Sunday school and afterwards to serve for years as one of the four altar boys.

Where I lived I learned that to set foot into the front door of St Joseph's Catholic Church meant to plunge straight down to hell! Some of my best childhood friends were catholic. Ron Konetchy, a year older and an accomplished musician was a special friend even into our later years. Two other close friends with whom I played golf and basketball were of the Catholic faith. Needless to say it was confusing. Ron's mom 'Sis' Konetchy owned the local bakery where on a cold winter morn I knew I could always stop and find the half dozen chocolate cupcakes on the top of the counter in a pink box waiting for me for my breakfast. Catholic, yes, and I could always count on her.

Ron has been gone for sometime now but he served in the US Navy, graduated from Yale and I had the good fortune to travel with him, the Yale Alumni Choir and the Waterbury Choral throughout China as their spokesperson on Central China National TV.

Chapter 28

"Give'em Hell Harry"

My God how things have changed in my lifetime. Innocence of that past is gone, lost.

I entered college after I graduated from Rushford High School. While at college The President of the United Stated States, Harry Truman was campaigning for reelection and was "on the stump" as was then the term. This was an occasion we could not miss so three of my college pals and I planned to be early and close to the tracks so we could see our president.

The four of us waited and as the train slowed to a stop in Winona, Minnesota we were positioned immediately behind the caboose. The rear door opened and out onto the platform stepped our dapper President. His gaze covered the group behind the train. He had a steely look with grey hair and glasses somewhat low on his nose. There was no doubt that he was in charge.

I do not recall a presence of security nor did we think of it in those days. The President stepped to the railing, put his hands around the top rail, looked straight down over the top of his glasses at us and spoke of the state of the nation. He was a straight arrow guy, no baloney. I recall now that some real tough decisions were made during his tenure in office. The bottom line, we were no more than six feet from our President. As the train began moving away, "Give'em Hell Harry." could be heard from the small group of college freshmen on the tracks and it brought a twinkle to his eye.

Chapter 29

Jiggs and Pea Vines

I was in college and Mom and Hugo had once again relocated, this time to Stockton, a tiny village in the southeast area of the state. There were only a handful of business establishments to see as one drove through this small town. It was truly one of those blink your eyes and you will miss it towns. Hugo and mom moved into a small old abandoned commercial building on a corner. Once again, the sum total of their earthly possessions fit into the rear seat and trunk of the car.

For me it was a break in the harvest season of the pea crop in Plainview, Minnesota where I worked. A friend that had a car gave me a ride on his way home and dropped me off in front of the old building in Stockton. I knocked at the front door hoping I had the right location. The instant canine response from inside made me step backwards, miss the step and land on my backside. I know that bark. I called out Jiggs! The tone immediately changed. The little Boston terrier knew that his old pal was outside and the sounds changed to whining and howling. It had been some time since he had been in his favorite place, on my lap. Now, my little mutt could not wait to reunite, but it was not meant to be. No one answered the door. I hated to leave the little guy.

Knowing that Mom and Hugo were no doubt at the local tavern, just a block away I headed in that direction. There were about a half dozen cars parked to the side and in front of the building. New ownership and grand opening covered the windows of the storefront. I stood in front of the entrance before entering. I thought, *My God! Here we are again.* It looked like it would be a repeat chapter in my life. The beer sign over the front door blinking its message like so many of the past locations where I had spent too many days. Thought flashing back to my childhood overwhelmed me. I caught my breath, turned the knob and entered. The interior was almost a carbon copy of all the past taverns. With closed eyes one could be aware of their location. The stale beer and cigarette odor was overpowering but I needed to be with Jiggs so I entered. No one seemed glad to see me so I got the key and hurried back to Jiggs. It was worth it all just to have my friend greet me.

Jiggs had a love hate relationship with fire engines from an early age. He came home beat and bruised more times than I could count. A few days later a person who lived in the small town of Stockton came to the bar and said they had seen Jiggs alongside the road just outside of town and he was hurt. I took a box and headed up the road to retrieve him. The fire engine had finally ended his life.

It was summer and soon I went back to my job at the pea factory in the small town nearby to make money for the next year at college. I shared a room with other workers. We worked long days in the pea factory and smelled like rotting pea vines when we finished for the day. If you have never smelled rotting pea vines you are fortunate. That smell travels for miles around the area.

Chapter 30

Go West Young Man

to……..California!

An acquaintance of Hugo and Mom had gone to California and wrote back about jobs available and encouraged them to make the trip and so we did. I crawled in the backseat of the car stuffed in between our meager belongings and we headed for California.

When we arrived after days of travel we moved into a tiny apartment. I immediately sought employment. Finally Hugo went to work for Pyrex and I had a job at the mattress factory where our friend was a foreman.

The tiny apartment above the garage behind the main house was a welcome sight after eight hours of stapling box springs. I sprinted up the rickety metal steps and entered the screen door. It was really hot and humid. Mom was sprawled on the single couch in a scanty nightie with cigarette in hand and smoke curling out of her nose. Her pallid grey face with bright red lipstick was grotesque and betrayed her physical condition. I could not help but feel sorry for her.

"Go to the refrigerator and get yourself a cold beer." She commanded. The can was ice cold and when I popped the tab the cold beer flowed down my arm.

It was Friday and Hooks had stopped at the nearest watering hole to soak up a few beers with the boys. It was also payday and I had stopped at a bank to cash my check. Mom was watching as I counted the bills and set aside seventy four dollars for my part of the rent. The cold beer felt good as I finished the last swallow. Mom's eyes followed me as I entered their bedroom. I opened the top drawer and grasped the small leather box hidden in the back where I kept my savings. After several months I had plans to open a savings account at the local bank. I had failed to carry out the plan feeling my secret hiding place was safe. I heard the screen door slam shut and I greeted Hooks who had a six pack under his arm.

"Have a beer boy." Hooks muttered and generously popped the top.

Mom gestured to come to her side and passed me one of her favorite cigarettes. A few years ago she had taught me how to smoke. "You want to be a man don't you?" she asked.

Time passed and the room was dense with cigarette smoke and the smell of beer. Mom staggered to her feet, took a step toward the bathroom then began to spin in a circle and collapsed, her legs twisted and jerked. Her tongue was hanging loosely from a wide open mouth and eyes rolling in opposite directions. Hooks, who was always sure he knew everything said, "She had too much beer."

He dragged mom back to the couch and with his huge arms picked her up and laid her on the couch.

I found a pillow and eventually fell asleep on the floor.

The next morning loud knocking woke all three of us.

"Come in." Hooks ordered.

A strange man entered and said, "You have failed to make three car payments and you must pay or give me the keys."

Hooks muttered, "I now have a job at the soap factory in South Gate and will catch up."

The man had no patience as he demanded, "Pay me now or give me the keys."

I knew Hooks was really a deadbeat, but I didn't want anyone to say it so I stood up and shouted, "How much?"

"Ninety dollars!"

Once again Mom's eyes followed me to the dresser. She watched as I counted out ninety dollars. I still had more than one hundred that I stashed back in the leather box.

I stood up as straight as I could, handed the money to the man shouting, "Here is ninety dollars, now get out!"

I felt a little like a hero for pulling those two out of an embarrassing experience. Honor thy mother and father! All these years I have tried though I know not why. My poor father never had a chance to know me nor did I know him before he succumbed at 31. Hugo had never really been a father.

After everything calmed down I got ready to leave.

"Mom I have a date tonight." I said as I sipped on a cup of coffee.

I was 20 years old. There was no mother and son affection, no bond.

This would be my second date and I wanted to make a good impression. I planned to take her to a Modern Jazz Quartet concert at the Lighthouse in Redondo Beach.. The tickets were eight dollars. I opened the stop dresser drawer and reached into the right rear for the leather box. Panic! It had been removed. A search found it under a pair of socks but the box was empty. I felt like vomiting.

"More coffee?" was Mom's command as she reached for the cup.

Honor thy Mother and father kept me from asking them, but I asked myself, *Where is the money?*

The knock on the door I knew was my friend from work. "Let's go." he stressed. He had a car and was my only transportation. I almost ran to the car and we were off to Manhattan Beach.

She was waiting at the door of a house she shared with other girls.

"I'm sorry I'm late!" I stated.

"OK." was her cheerful reply.

"I can't stay. I am sorry. I lost all my money and can't buy the tickets." I was mortified to admit it and face the fact that I was a loser. I thought, *You will never see her again.*

She reached for my hand and said, "I have money, I cashed my check from the telephone company. Let me buy the tickets." The evening was embarrassing but enjoyable.

Afterward my friend drove back and stopped the car near the front door of the apartment where I lived. It was midnight when I ran up the stairs as quietly as possible. I at the top of the stairs I turned the key in the lock and opened the door with some hesitation.

Hooks stood in the kitchen, a bottle of Hamm's beer in one hand and an Old Gold cigarette in the other and he said, "Our little mummy passed away tonight."

He took a pack of Old Gold from his shirt pocket, tapped it on his hand as cigarette smokers do, and offered me the single smoke. I put the cigarette in my mouth and accepted the light he offered. I took a deep drag on the Old Gold with smoke curling up through my nose.

In retrospect, after decades, I think of how incredibly cold I had responded. Actually, that was the true depth of my feeling.

Hooks went to the refrigerator, popped open two cans of beer, handed one to me and we had a beer and a cigarette.

Hooks explained that she had had another seizure, was taken to a charity hospital where she died from a brain tumor without ever recovering consciousness.

Finally he asked, "What do you want to do?

My silence was no help but my thoughts were that she would want to be buried in the family plot back in Minnesota. According to what little I knew, my father's parents had a plot and my mother's parents had a different plot as separated in death as they had always been in life.

Hooks looked at me with question and said, "Probably a funeral in the Rushford Lutheran Church would be appropriate."

I was quiet. I did not know who took the meager savings out of the little leather box after I paid the man that came to repossess the car. Was it Mom or Hooks? I still do not know. I only knew I was dead broke with a dead mother, and no place to go.

Hooks questioned, "Go back to Minnesota?"

"NO!"

It took several days to get the money. The factory where I worked took money from my pay check. We shipped the body by train back to the town of her birth. Hugo accompanied her. The funeral was conducted in the great stone church and burial in the family plot, the plot of her parents.

Almost everyone in this small town has a safety net. Family! If all fails for a person, somebody in the family is usually there to pick up the pieces, lend a hand and help them through the crisis. It is like a family warranty program. Sometime in my past that bond was broken for me. While I have many relatives, I have never had a family system and must continue fly alone.

I am daily reminded of the vacuum I grew up in.

Chapter 31

Who the Hell Cares!

The new Toyota Camry glided silently next to the curb in my small Midwestern home town and I was back again. The dust that the car had disturbed was just beginning to settle. Dried mud from the flood of 2007 coated all horizontal surfaces and vertical areas up to four feet high in Rushford.

It was just a few days after the calamitous flood had swept over my little Minnesota hometown. There had been floods before but there had never in the past been such a deluge. Surprisingly it was Rush Creek not the Root River that overflowed the dike system installed by the Corps of Engineers.

It had been a flood of Biblical proportions, leaving countless homes ruined. Many houses were condemned and doomed to destruction in this small town of less than 2000 people. There had been twelve inches of rain in the previous week, then, in one twenty four hour period, the sky dropped seventeen inches more. The deluge funneled its way off the high flat ridges above the valley, down the steep bluff sides into the junction of the Root River and Rush Creek.

This small town has variously named Burroughs. The areas called Brooklyn, (across Rush Creek), Jerusalem (the lowest point), Pickle Alley and downtown. These areas were the hardest hit. People described running for their lives in the water as it rose around them or being rescued out of second story windows from their homes clothed in their pajamas. One person had to be rescued by chopping a hole in the roof to pull her out. This all happened in the dark of night. Some described glancing back to see the water rushing and rising like a small tsunami.

Mold! Somebody said Mold! It was treated as a new plague. People seemed to panic. Mold in many of its forms had been in the location far longer than any of its human inhabitants. The sudden suggestion of a fungus brought on a new awareness of a sniffle, a new headache, a pimple or a symptom of a possible life threatening malady or previous undiscovered areas of physical weakness. Others were searching for sympathy or maybe an excuse. Throw away everything became the cry! Huge piles of debris, furniture, lumber and metal though usable if cleaned were hauled away as trash.

At some time in the past the Army Corps of Engineers had designed and installed a dike system to protect the town but once the water got into the city the dike kept it from getting out. It took farm equipment three days to pump the city dry. In the past the Root River had brought flood waters many times. The water would go up, flood the town and then recede and the citizens would shovel mud, scrub the floors and walls, paint and resume life as it had been. New regulations now strangled the town. Houses, homes that had previously survived decades of floods were now condemned and doomed to destruction because the water sat in the town for three days before it was all pumped out.

411 Grove Street (photo by M. Holle)

Now I am standing before the mailbox with the number 411 Grove Street printed but somewhat worn, on the face of the metal container. It is the address stamped on my birth certificate. The little red flag sadly hung down indicating there was no mail. The last delivery had been made. It would be a long time before any mail would or if ever be delivered to that address. I raised my gaze to the front of the small white dwelling, its front door gaping open as though someone left, had given up, was gone and never coming back. The flow of dried mud covering the floor showed through the opening. The two holes on each side of the front door had obviously been windows blown out by the force of the water. This was the house that had been rented by my father and mother when they were first married.

Hidden in this house are the mysterious details of our three lives. I was born somewhere within those four walls over seventy seven years ago on a warm day in July at about 11:00 in the morning. Though I had seen the house from the outside on visits back to Rushford while living in California, I could not in my memory recall ever being inside with my father and mother in a normal family setting. I felt strange vibes.

I walked to the rear. There was the old shed still leaning as it always had been in my memory, during periods of passing by and being drawn to glancing in that direction.

I approached and hesitated before entering the leaning and twisted back door of the house. I stood slowly glancing to the right and the left and then moving forward into the open back door. I heard the floor emit soft sounds. The thick drying mud covered the entire floor surface. On the left were obviously two bedrooms, both small, one a little larger than the other. They were separated by a tiny bathroom. On the right was the small kitchen. Ahead I could see the living room, though I doubt if living room was a term used when the little house was built, it was most likely called the parlor. A small nook was probably a dining area. There were signs of ancient wallpaper and floor covering. To me it was a house of mystery.

What were their lives like when my father and mother lived in this little white house?

I had heard small bits of information from relatives later in life. I barely knew about the unusual circumstances. My father was the only son of a prominent local business man. My mother was the youngest daughter of a local alcoholic who treated his family of twelve badly. There must have been times of great strife in my maternal grandfather's house. My mother was considered from the other side of the tracks, so to speak, the last of twelve children of an alcoholic, one of the dregs of life, and not an acceptable choice for the son of Albert and Marie.

I know not when the tenancy of the dwelling began or was ended; I only know that somewhere in that house I opened my eyes for the first time. My father and mother must have been delighted at my arrival. I was to be their first and only child.

One thing is certain those early days after my first breath were not of the ordinary. The temporary residence rented by mom and dad where I was born was just a moment in time. The tiny dwelling must have stood the ravages of time and weather looking unchanged for years.

I hesitated and looked back over my shoulder as I was exiting the front door. Was I born in the back or middle bedroom? It was really not important, just in a small way…. to me. It was modest, modest was an understatement. It was not just a house, it had been a home. My first home, it was my birthplace and it was about to be relegated into oblivion as were much of the circumstances of my early childhood. I knew I would never come back.

I exited the front door. A quick look over my left shoulder and adios. Now, it is but a short time before the bulldozer will arrive and with one single sweep, the house and shed will pass into history.

Out on the front lawn I had to look back. Why, I don't know. It had always been painted white as I remember passing it in my childhood. As a child I remember it looking bigger. It looked sad with the chipped peeling paint and shingles on the roof curling and bare. Sad, as were the circumstances of my childhood. Perhaps, the flood merely set the final time. It soon would have collapsed from decades of disrepair and neglect. The post of the mailbox was leaning to the west, but the numbers 411 still were clear on the box and, indicated the location on the street in the Brooklyn section of Rushford.

I looked down the street, piles of trash and empty spaces filled my teary eyes, spaces where homes and families existed only a month ago. Gone. Change was and is the only constant.

Something that some of us do not want to consider. Wherever, some of us that were born here had traveled in the past, we probably had no doubt that Rushford would always be there for us as it was, as it had always been.

The two tall pine trees in the front yard stood unmoved by the events of the previous days. These trees had lived through many weather events over decades and remained unchanged, while the human inhabitants suffered, but ultimately both staunchly survived. The trees hopefully will always be there for someone to see long after all of us pass.

The sound of heavy machinery approaching caught my attention. Now sitting in the car getting my last look I turned and watched as the large yellow machine came down the street turned right, ran beside the 411 mailbox and between the two great old pines. It looked like a huge monster praying mantis.

Directly in front of the house it set the two front and rear stationary points. Then the great arm rose into the air. It hesitated and the jaws parted. I heard the squeak and squeal of the arm as it plunged the huge teeth into the front half of the house filling the air with dust. The jaws closed and the arm raised, it swung around and the rubble was dropped into the waiting dump truck. The next few scoops removed any and all of the house where I was born. A personal history was erased. Ultimately, weather, time, flood and machinery claimed their prize and the only trace of the dwelling is a rather small hole in the ground that had been a cellar on an otherwise empty lot, unkempt with weeds rising here and there around it. I decided to visit the Lutheran Cemetery where I knew my relatives were buried so I headed out of town. It was only a few miles in reality but it seemed like I was travelling back ages in time. I walked past many names I remembered from my childhood until I found the two family names I was seeking. They were in far separated areas. We were there looking at where my relatives are buried when my little dog stepped up and started to piss on my mother's grave. I looked around to see if anyone was watching and then I just let her finish.

What happened? It was personal tragedy. *"Stop whining!* I tell myself. *I am alive and well?"*

I daily try to shove all of this into that area of non-recall in my mind. I was looking forward as I drove out of Rushford, but I had to look back just for a last glimpse in my rear view mirror and said aloud, *"Who the hell cares.?"*

THE END

Would you like to see your manuscript become a book?

If you are interested in becoming a PublishAmerica author, please submit your manuscript for possible publication to us at:

acquisitions@publishamerica.com

You may also mail in your manuscript to:

**PublishAmerica
PO Box 151
Frederick, MD 21705**

www.publishamerica.com

CPSIA information can be obtained at www.ICGtesting.com
Printed in the USA
BVOW072217170412

287929BV00001B/39/P